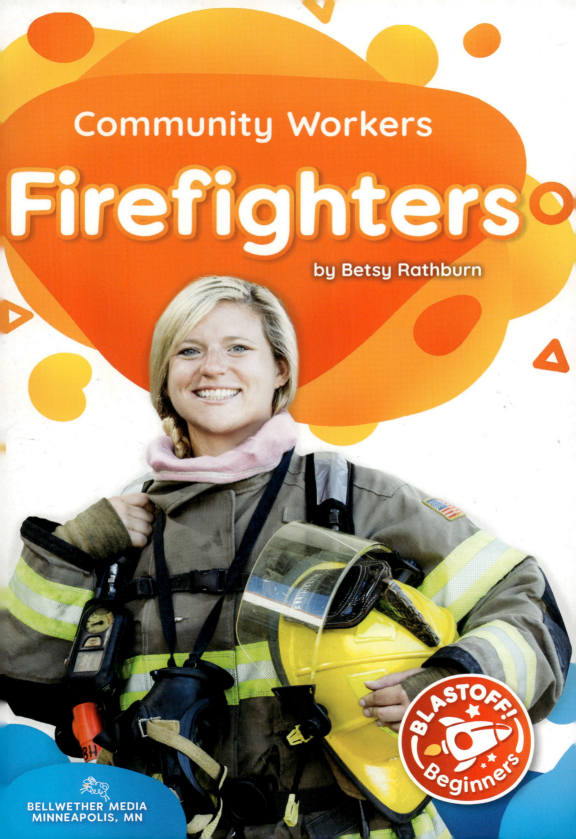

**Blastoff! Beginners** are developed by literacy experts and educators to meet the needs of early readers. These engaging informational texts support young children as they begin reading about their world. Through simple language and high frequency words paired with crisp, colorful photos, Blastoff! Beginners launch young readers into the universe of independent reading.

## Sight Words in This Book

| a | away | in | people | up |
| an | from | is | then | water |
| and | help | on | they | |
| are | here | out | to | |

This edition first published in 2025 by Bellwether Media, Inc.

No part of this publication may be reproduced in whole or in part without written permission of the publisher. For information regarding permission, write to Bellwether Media, Inc., Attention: Permissions Department, 6012 Blue Circle Drive, Minnetonka, MN 55343.

Library of Congress Cataloging-in-Publication Data

Names: Rathburn, Betsy, author.
Title: Firefighters / by Betsy Rathburn.
Description: Minneapolis, MN : Bellwether Media, Inc. 2025. | Series: Blastoff! beginners: community helpers | Includes bibliographical references and index. | Audience: Ages 4-7 | Audience: Grades K-1 |
  Summary: "Developed by literacy experts and educators for students in PreK through grade two, this book introduces beginning readers to firefighters through simple, predictable text and related photos"--Provided by publisher.
Identifiers: LCCN 2024004955 (print) | LCCN 2024004956 (ebook) | ISBN 9798886870084 (library binding) | ISBN 9781644878453 (ebook)
Subjects: LCSH: Fire extinction--Juvenile literature. | Fire fighters--Juvenile literature.
Classification: LCC TH9148 .R37 2025  (print) | LCC TH9148  (ebook) | DDC 363.37092--dc23/eng/20240212
LC record available at https://lccn.loc.gov/2024004955
LC ebook record available at https://lccn.loc.gov/2024004956

Text copyright © 2025 by Bellwether Media, Inc. BLASTOFF! BEGINNERS and associated logos are trademarks and/or registered trademarks of Bellwether Media, Inc. Bellwether Media is a division of Chrysalis Education Group.

Editor: Rebecca Sabelko    Designer: Laura Sowers

Printed in the United States of America, North Mankato, MN.

# Table of Contents

| On the Job | 4 |
| --- | --- |
| What Are They? | 6 |
| What Do They Do? | 12 |
| Why Do We Need Them? | 20 |
| Firefighter Facts | 22 |
| Glossary | 23 |
| To Learn More | 24 |
| Index | 24 |

# On the Job

A building is on fire. Firefighters are here to help!

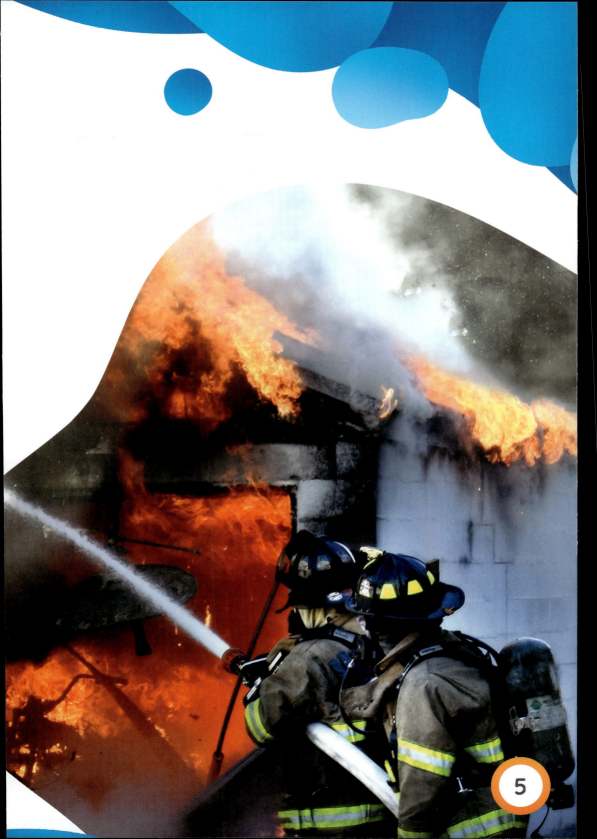

# What Are They?

Firefighters are brave workers. They help in **emergencies**.

They put out fires. They save people from danger.

They work in cities and towns. They stay in **fire stations**.

fire station

# What Do They Do?

Ding, ding! An **alarm** rings. Firefighters race to help!

alarm

They wear heavy clothing. Then they speed away on a fire truck!

They set up ladders. They climb to save people!

They pull out **hoses**.
They spray water on fires!

## Why Do We Need Them?

Firefighters face danger. They keep us safe!

# Firefighter Facts

## Tools

heavy clothing

hose

ladder

## A Day in the Life

ride in a fire truck

climb ladders

spray water on fires

# Glossary

**alarm**

a loud sound to warn of danger

**emergencies**

times when people need quick help

**fire stations**

places where firefighters wait for emergencies

**hoses**

long tubes that spray water

# To Learn More

## ON THE WEB

# FACTSURFER

Factsurfer.com gives you a safe, fun way to find more information.

1. Go to www.factsurfer.com.

2. Enter "firefighters" into the search box and click 🔍.

3. Select your book cover to see a list of related content.

# Index

alarm, 12
brave, 6
building, 4
cities, 10
climb, 16
clothing, 14
danger, 8, 20

emergencies, 6
fire, 4, 8, 18
fire stations, 10
fire truck, 14
help, 4, 6, 12

hoses, 18, 19
ladders, 16, 17
people, 8, 16
save, 8, 16
towns, 10
water, 18
work, 10

The images in this book are reproduced through the courtesy of: kali9, front cover, pp. 20-21; Grigvovan, p. 3; Scott Anderson Photo, pp. 4-5; MarkCoffeyPhoto, pp. 6-7; Quadxeon, pp. 8-9; Pierre-Olivier, p. 10 (fire station); Johner Images/ Alamy, pp. 10-11; Neung Day, p. 12 (alarm); xavierarnau, pp. 12-13; Flashon Studio, pp. 14, 22 (heavy clothes); blurAZ, pp. 14-15; Steve_Jolicoeur/ Alamy, pp. 16-17; Gregory Simpson, pp. 17-18; serhii.suravikin, p. 22 (hose); Kues, p. 22 (ladder); AzmanL, p. 22 (ride in a fire truck); Steve Sanchez Photos, p. 22 (climb ladders); TFoxFoto, p. 22 (spray water on fires); Aleksandr Grechanyuk, p. 23 (alarm); MAGNIFIER, p. 23 (emergencies); Eddie J. Rodriquez, p. 23 (fire stations); Digital Art StudioTH, p. 23 (hoses).